Monthly Bill
Payment Tracker

This Books Belongs To

_____

_____

BANK ACCOUNT INFORMATION

ACCOUNT NAME

BANK NAME:	ACCOUNT TYPE:
ACCOUNT NUMBER:	ROUTING NUMBER:
USERNAME:	PASSWORD:
DEBIT CARD NUMBER:	PIN NUMBER:
ADDRESS:	
NOTES:	

ACCOUNT NAME

BANK NAME:	ACCOUNT TYPE:
ACCOUNT NUMBER:	ROUTING NUMBER:
USERNAME:	PASSWORD:
DEBIT CARD NUMBER:	PIN NUMBER:
ADDRESS:	
NOTES:	

ACCOUNT NAME

BANK NAME:	ACCOUNT TYPE:
ACCOUNT NUMBER:	ROUTING NUMBER:
USERNAME:	PASSWORD:
DEBIT CARD NUMBER:	PIN NUMBER:
ADDRESS:	
NOTES:	

BANK ACCOUNT INFORMATION

ACCOUNT NAME

BANK NAME:	ACCOUNT TYPE:
ACCOUNT NUMBER:	ROUTING NUMBER:
USERNAME:	PASSWORD:
DEBIT CARD NUMBER:	PIN NUMBER:
ADDRESS:	
NOTES:	

ACCOUNT NAME

BANK NAME:	ACCOUNT TYPE:
ACCOUNT NUMBER:	ROUTING NUMBER:
USERNAME:	PASSWORD:
DEBIT CARD NUMBER:	PIN NUMBER:
ADDRESS:	
NOTES:	

ACCOUNT NAME

BANK NAME:	ACCOUNT TYPE:
ACCOUNT NUMBER:	ROUTING NUMBER:
USERNAME:	PASSWORD:
DEBIT CARD NUMBER:	PIN NUMBER:
ADDRESS:	
NOTES:	

My Yearly Financial Goals

1

2

3

4

5

6

7

8

My Mind Map

Month / Year: _____

| Jan | Feb | Mar | Apr | May | Jun | Jul | Aug | Sep | Oct | Nov | Dec |

Starting Balance: _____

INCOME

DATE	SOURCE	AMOUNT
	TOTAL	

This Month's Goals

- ■ _____
- ■ _____
- ■ _____
- ■ _____
- ■ _____

INCOME

DATE	DESCRIPTION	AMOUNT
	TOTAL	

BILLS & FIXED EXPENSES

DUE	DESCRIPTION	AMOUNT
	TOTAL	

DEBT

DATE	DESCRIPTION	AMOUNT
	TOTAL	

Month / Year: _____ | Jan | Feb | Mar | Apr | May | Jun | Jul | Aug | Sep | Oct | Nov | Dec |

Starting Balance: _____

INCOME		
DATE	SOURCE	AMOUNT
	TOTAL	

This Month's Goals

- ■ _____
- ■ _____
- ■ _____
- ■ _____
- ■ _____

INCOME		
DATE	DESCRIPTION	AMOUNT
	TOTAL	

BILLS & FIXED EXPENSES		
DUE	DESCRIPTION	AMOUNT
	TOTAL	

DEBT		
DATE	DESCRIPTION	AMOUNT
	TOTAL	

Monthly Bill Payment

PAID	BILL	DUE DATE	AMT. DUE	AMT. PAID	UNPAID BALANCE	NOTES
Total						

THIS MONTH'S FINANCIAL OVERVIEW

OPENING BALANCE	
TOTAL INCOME	
TOTAL EXPENSES	
DIFFERENCE	
TOTAL SAVINGS	
BALANCE FORWARD	

MY BIGGEST SPENDING AREA

MY SMALLEST SPENDING AREA

Month / Year: _____ | Jan | Feb | Mar | Apr | May | Jun | Jul | Aug | Sep | Oct | Nov | Dec |

Starting Balance: _____

INCOME		
DATE	SOURCE	AMOUNT
	TOTAL	

This Month's Goals
■ _____
■ _____
■ _____
■ _____
■ _____

INCOME		
DATE	DESCRIPTION	AMOUNT
	TOTAL	

BILLS & FIXED EXPENSES		
DUE	DESCRIPTION	AMOUNT
	TOTAL	

DEBT		
DATE	DESCRIPTION	AMOUNT
	TOTAL	

Monthly Bill Payment

PAID	BILL	DUE DATE	AMT. DUE	AMT. PAID	UNPAID BALANCE	NOTES
	Total					

THIS MONTH'S FINANCIAL OVERVIEW

OPENING BALANCE	
TOTAL INCOME	
TOTAL EXPENSES	
DIFFERENCE	
TOTAL SAVINGS	
BALANCE FORWARD	

MY BIGGEST SPENDING AREA

MY SMALLEST SPENDING AREA

Month / Year: _____

| Jan | Feb | Mar | Apr | May | Jun | Jul | Aug | Sep | Oct | Nov | Dec |

Starting Balance: _____

INCOME

DATE	SOURCE	AMOUNT
	TOTAL	

This Month's Goals

■ _____

■ _____

■ _____

■ _____

■ _____

INCOME

DATE	DESCRIPTION	AMOUNT
	TOTAL	

BILLS & FIXED EXPENSES

DUE	DESCRIPTION	AMOUNT
	TOTAL	

DEBT

DATE	DESCRIPTION	AMOUNT
	TOTAL	

Monthly Bill Payment

PAID	BILL	DUE DATE	AMT. DUE	AMT. PAID	UNPAID BALANCE	NOTES
	Total					

THIS MONTH'S FINANCIAL OVERVIEW

OPENING BALANCE	
TOTAL INCOME	
TOTAL EXPENSES	
DIFFERENCE	
TOTAL SAVINGS	
BALANCE FORWARD	

MY BIGGEST SPENDING AREA

MY SMALLEST SPENDING AREA

Month / Year: _____ | Jan | Feb | Mar | Apr | May | Jun | Jul | Aug | Sep | Oct | Nov | Dec

Starting Balance: _____

INCOME

DATE	SOURCE	AMOUNT
	TOTAL	

This Month's Goals

- ■ _____
- ■ _____
- ■ _____
- ■ _____
- ■ _____

INCOME

DATE	DESCRIPTION	AMOUNT
	TOTAL	

BILLS & FIXED EXPENSES

DUE	DESCRIPTION	AMOUNT
	TOTAL	

DEBT

DATE	DESCRIPTION	AMOUNT
	TOTAL	

Monthly Bill Payment

PAID	BILL	DUE DATE	AMT. DUE	AMT. PAID	UNPAID BALANCE	NOTES
Total						

THIS MONTH'S FINANCIAL OVERVIEW

OPENING BALANCE	
TOTAL INCOME	
TOTAL EXPENSES	
DIFFERENCE	
TOTAL SAVINGS	
BALANCE FORWARD	

MY BIGGEST SPENDING AREA

MY SMALLEST SPENDING AREA

Month / Year: _____ | Jan | Feb | Mar | Apr | May | Jun | Jul | Aug | Sep | Oct | Nov | Dec |

Starting Balance: _____

INCOME

DATE	SOURCE	AMOUNT
	TOTAL	

This Month's Goals

- ■ _____
- ■ _____
- ■ _____
- ■ _____
- ■ _____

INCOME

DATE	DESCRIPTION	AMOUNT
	TOTAL	

BILLS & FIXED EXPENSES

DUE	DESCRIPTION	AMOUNT
	TOTAL	

DEBT

DATE	DESCRIPTION	AMOUNT
	TOTAL	

Monthly Bill Payment

PAID	BILL	DUE DATE	AMT. DUE	AMT. PAID	UNPAID BALANCE	NOTES
Total						

THIS MONTH'S FINANCIAL OVERVIEW

OPENING BALANCE	
TOTAL INCOME	
TOTAL EXPENSES	
DIFFERENCE	
TOTAL SAVINGS	
BALANCE FORWARD	

MY BIGGEST SPENDING AREA

MY SMALLEST SPENDING AREA

Month / Year: _____

| Jan | Feb | Mar | Apr | May | Jun | Jul | Aug | Sep | Oct | Nov | Dec |

Starting Balance: _____

INCOME

DATE	SOURCE	AMOUNT
	TOTAL	

This Month's Goals

- ▪ _____
- ▪ _____
- ▪ _____
- ▪ _____
- ▪ _____

INCOME

DATE	DESCRIPTION	AMOUNT
	TOTAL	

BILLS & FIXED EXPENSES

DUE	DESCRIPTION	AMOUNT
	TOTAL	

DEBT

DATE	DESCRIPTION	AMOUNT
	TOTAL	

Monthly Bill Payment

PAID	BILL	DUE DATE	AMT. DUE	AMT. PAID	UNPAID BALANCE	NOTES
Total						

THIS MONTH'S FINANCIAL OVERVIEW

OPENING BALANCE	
TOTAL INCOME	
TOTAL EXPENSES	
DIFFERENCE	
TOTAL SAVINGS	
BALANCE FORWARD	

MY BIGGEST SPENDING AREA

MY SMALLEST SPENDING AREA

Month / Year: _____

| Jan | Feb | Mar | Apr | May | Jun | Jul | Aug | Sep | Oct | Nov | Dec |

Starting Balance: _____

INCOME

DATE	SOURCE	AMOUNT
	TOTAL	

This Month's Goals

- ■ _____
- ■ _____
- ■ _____
- ■ _____
- ■ _____

INCOME

DATE	DESCRIPTION	AMOUNT
	TOTAL	

BILLS & FIXED EXPENSES

DUE	DESCRIPTION	AMOUNT
	TOTAL	

DEBT

DATE	DESCRIPTION	AMOUNT
	TOTAL	

Monthly Bill Payment

OTHER BILLS & EXPENSES

PAID	BILL	DUE DATE	AMT. DUE	AMT. PAID	UNPAID BALANCE	NOTES
Total						

THIS MONTH'S FINANCIAL OVERVIEW

OPENING BALANCE	
TOTAL INCOME	
TOTAL EXPENSES	
DIFFERENCE	
TOTAL SAVINGS	
BALANCE FORWARD	

MY BIGGEST SPENDING AREA

MY SMALLEST SPENDING AREA

Month / Year: _____

| Jan | Feb | Mar | Apr | May | Jun | Jul | Aug | Sep | Oct | Nov | Dec |

| Starting Balance: _____ |

INCOME

DATE	SOURCE	AMOUNT
	TOTAL	

This Month's Goals

- ■ _____
- ■ _____
- ■ _____
- ■ _____
- ■ _____

INCOME

DATE	DESCRIPTION	AMOUNT
	TOTAL	

BILLS & FIXED EXPENSES

DUE	DESCRIPTION	AMOUNT
	TOTAL	

DEBT

DATE	DESCRIPTION	AMOUNT
	TOTAL	

Monthly Bill Payment

PAID	BILL	DUE DATE	AMT. DUE	AMT. PAID	UNPAID BALANCE	NOTES
	Total					

THIS MONTH'S FINANCIAL OVERVIEW

OPENING BALANCE	
TOTAL INCOME	
TOTAL EXPENSES	
DIFFERENCE	
TOTAL SAVINGS	
BALANCE FORWARD	

MY BIGGEST SPENDING AREA

MY SMALLEST SPENDING AREA

Month / Year: _____ | Jan | Feb | Mar | Apr | May | Jun | Jul | Aug | Sep | Oct | Nov | Dec

Starting Balance: _____

INCOME

DATE	SOURCE	AMOUNT
	TOTAL	

This Month's Goals

- ■ _____
- ■ _____
- ■ _____
- ■ _____
- ■ _____

INCOME

DATE	DESCRIPTION	AMOUNT
	TOTAL	

BILLS & FIXED EXPENSES

DUE	DESCRIPTION	AMOUNT
	TOTAL	

DEBT

DATE	DESCRIPTION	AMOUNT
	TOTAL	

Monthly Bill Payment

PAID	BILL	DUE DATE	AMT. DUE	AMT. PAID	UNPAID BALANCE	NOTES
	Total					

THIS MONTH'S FINANCIAL OVERVIEW

OPENING BALANCE	
TOTAL INCOME	
TOTAL EXPENSES	
DIFFERENCE	
TOTAL SAVINGS	
BALANCE FORWARD	

MY BIGGEST SPENDING AREA

MY SMALLEST SPENDING AREA

Month / Year: _____

| Jan | Feb | Mar | Apr | May | Jun | Jul | Aug | Sep | Oct | Nov | Dec |

Starting Balance: _____

INCOME		
DATE	SOURCE	AMOUNT
	TOTAL	

This Month's Goals

- ▪ _____
- ▪ _____
- ▪ _____
- ▪ _____
- ▪ _____

INCOME		
DATE	DESCRIPTION	AMOUNT
	TOTAL	

BILLS & FIXED EXPENSES		
DUE	DESCRIPTION	AMOUNT
	TOTAL	

DEBT		
DATE	DESCRIPTION	AMOUNT
	TOTAL	

Monthly Bill Payment

OTHER BILLS & EXPENSES

PAID	BILL	DUE DATE	AMT. DUE	AMT. PAID	UNPAID BALANCE	NOTES
	Total					

THIS MONTH'S FINANCIAL OVERVIEW

OPENING BALANCE	
TOTAL INCOME	
TOTAL EXPENSES	
DIFFERENCE	
TOTAL SAVINGS	
BALANCE FORWARD	

MY BIGGEST SPENDING AREA

MY SMALLEST SPENDING AREA

Month / Year: _____ | Jan | Feb | Mar | Apr | May | Jun | Jul | Aug | Sep | Oct | Nov | Dec

Starting Balance: _____

INCOME

DATE	SOURCE	AMOUNT
	TOTAL	

This Month's Goals

- ◼ _____
- ◼ _____
- ◼ _____
- ◼ _____
- ◼ _____

INCOME

DATE	DESCRIPTION	AMOUNT
	TOTAL	

BILLS & FIXED EXPENSES

DUE	DESCRIPTION	AMOUNT
	TOTAL	

DEBT

DATE	DESCRIPTION	AMOUNT
	TOTAL	

Monthly Bill Payment

OTHER BILLS & EXPENSES

PAID	BILL	DUE DATE	AMT. DUE	AMT. PAID	UNPAID BALANCE	NOTES
	Total					

THIS MONTH'S FINANCIAL OVERVIEW

OPENING BALANCE	
TOTAL INCOME	
TOTAL EXPENSES	
DIFFERENCE	
TOTAL SAVINGS	
BALANCE FORWARD	

MY BIGGEST SPENDING AREA

MY SMALLEST SPENDING AREA

Month / Year: _____

| Jan | Feb | Mar | Apr | May | Jun | Jul | Aug | Sep | Oct | Nov | Dec |

Starting Balance: _____

INCOME

DATE	SOURCE	AMOUNT
	TOTAL	

This Month's Goals

- ☐ _____
- ☐ _____
- ☐ _____
- ☐ _____
- ☐ _____

INCOME

DATE	DESCRIPTION	AMOUNT
	TOTAL	

BILLS & FIXED EXPENSES

DUE	DESCRIPTION	AMOUNT
	TOTAL	

DEBT

DATE	DESCRIPTION	AMOUNT
	TOTAL	

Monthly Bill Payment

OTHER BILLS & EXPENSES

PAID	BILL	DUE DATE	AMT. DUE	AMT. PAID	UNPAID BALANCE	NOTES
	Total					

THIS MONTH'S FINANCIAL OVERVIEW

OPENING BALANCE	
TOTAL INCOME	
TOTAL EXPENSES	
DIFFERENCE	
TOTAL SAVINGS	
BALANCE FORWARD	

MY BIGGEST SPENDING AREA

MY SMALLEST SPENDING AREA

SUMMARY OF THE YEAR

MONTH	JAN	FEB	MAR	APR	APR	JUN
TOTAL INCOME						
TOTAL EXPENSES						
BALANCE						
SAVINGS						

Monthly Expenses Summary

CATEGORY	JAN	FEB	MAR	APR	APR	JUN

SUMMARY OF THE YEAR

MONTH	Jul	Aug	Sep	Oct	Nov	Dec
TOTAL INCOME						
TOTAL EXPENSES						
BALANCE						
SAVINGS						

Monthly Expenses Summary

CATEGORY	Jul	Aug	Sep	Oct	Nov	Dec

My Yearly Financial Goals

1

2

3

4

5

6

7

8

My Mind Map

Month / Year: _____ | Jan | Feb | Mar | Apr | May | Jun | Jul | Aug | Sep | Oct | Nov | Dec |

Starting Balance: _____

INCOME

DATE	SOURCE	AMOUNT
	TOTAL	

This Month's Goals

- ■ _____
- ■ _____
- ■ _____
- ■ _____
- ■ _____

INCOME

DATE	DESCRIPTION	AMOUNT
	TOTAL	

BILLS & FIXED EXPENSES

DUE	DESCRIPTION	AMOUNT
	TOTAL	

DEBT

DATE	DESCRIPTION	AMOUNT
	TOTAL	

Monthly Bill Payment

PAID	BILL	DUE DATE	AMT. DUE	AMT. PAID	UNPAID BALANCE	NOTES
Total						

THIS MONTH'S FINANCIAL OVERVIEW

OPENING BALANCE	
TOTAL INCOME	
TOTAL EXPENSES	
DIFFERENCE	
TOTAL SAVINGS	
BALANCE FORWARD	

MY BIGGEST SPENDING AREA

MY SMALLEST SPENDING AREA

Month / Year: _____

| Jan | Feb | Mar | Apr | May | Jun | Jul | Aug | Sep | Oct | Nov | Dec |

Starting Balance: _____

INCOME

DATE	SOURCE	AMOUNT
	TOTAL	

This Month's Goals

- ■ _____
- ■ _____
- ■ _____
- ■ _____
- ■ _____

INCOME

DATE	DESCRIPTION	AMOUNT
	TOTAL	

BILLS & FIXED EXPENSES

DUE	DESCRIPTION	AMOUNT
	TOTAL	

DEBT

DATE	DESCRIPTION	AMOUNT
	TOTAL	

Monthly Bill Payment

PAID	BILL	DUE DATE	AMT. DUE	AMT. PAID	UNPAID BALANCE	NOTES
	Total					

THIS MONTH'S FINANCIAL OVERVIEW

OPENING BALANCE	
TOTAL INCOME	
TOTAL EXPENSES	
DIFFERENCE	
TOTAL SAVINGS	
BALANCE FORWARD	

MY BIGGEST SPENDING AREA

MY SMALLEST SPENDING AREA

Month / Year: _____

| Jan | Feb | Mar | Apr | May | Jun | Jul | Aug | Sep | Oct | Nov | Dec |

Starting Balance: _____

INCOME

DATE	SOURCE	AMOUNT
	TOTAL	

This Month's Goals

- ■ _____
- ■ _____
- ■ _____
- ■ _____
- ■ _____

INCOME

DATE	DESCRIPTION	AMOUNT
	TOTAL	

BILLS & FIXED EXPENSES

DUE	DESCRIPTION	AMOUNT
	TOTAL	

DEBT

DATE	DESCRIPTION	AMOUNT
	TOTAL	

Monthly Bill Payment

PAID	BILL	DUE DATE	AMT. DUE	AMT. PAID	UNPAID BALANCE	NOTES
Total						

THIS MONTH'S FINANCIAL OVERVIEW

OPENING BALANCE	
TOTAL INCOME	
TOTAL EXPENSES	
DIFFERENCE	
TOTAL SAVINGS	
BALANCE FORWARD	

MY BIGGEST SPENDING AREA

MY SMALLEST SPENDING AREA

Month / Year: _____

| Jan | Feb | Mar | Apr | May | Jun | Jul | Aug | Sep | Oct | Nov | Dec |

| Starting Balance: _____ |

INCOME

DATE	SOURCE	AMOUNT
	TOTAL	

This Month's Goals

- ▪ _____
- ▪ _____
- ▪ _____
- ▪ _____
- ▪ _____

INCOME

DATE	DESCRIPTION	AMOUNT
	TOTAL	

BILLS & FIXED EXPENSES

DUE	DESCRIPTION	AMOUNT
	TOTAL	

DEBT

DATE	DESCRIPTION	AMOUNT
	TOTAL	

Monthly Bill Payment

PAID	BILL	DUE DATE	AMT. DUE	AMT. PAID	UNPAID BALANCE	NOTES
	Total					

THIS MONTH'S FINANCIAL OVERVIEW

OPENING BALANCE	
TOTAL INCOME	
TOTAL EXPENSES	
DIFFERENCE	
TOTAL SAVINGS	
BALANCE FORWARD	

MY BIGGEST SPENDING AREA

MY SMALLEST SPENDING AREA

Month / Year: _____

Jan Feb Mar Apr May Jun Jul Aug Sep Oct Nov Dec

Starting Balance: _____

INCOME

DATE	SOURCE	AMOUNT
	TOTAL	

This Month's Goals

- ☐ _____
- ☐ _____
- ☐ _____
- ☐ _____
- ☐ _____

INCOME

DATE	DESCRIPTION	AMOUNT
	TOTAL	

BILLS & FIXED EXPENSES

DUE	DESCRIPTION	AMOUNT
	TOTAL	

DEBT

DATE	DESCRIPTION	AMOUNT
	TOTAL	

Monthly Bill Payment

PAID	BILL	DUE DATE	AMT. DUE	AMT. PAID	UNPAID BALANCE	NOTES
	Total					

THIS MONTH'S FINANCIAL OVERVIEW

OPENING BALANCE	
TOTAL INCOME	
TOTAL EXPENSES	
DIFFERENCE	
TOTAL SAVINGS	
BALANCE FORWARD	

MY BIGGEST SPENDING AREA

MY SMALLEST SPENDING AREA

Month / Year: _____

Jan | Feb | Mar | Apr | May | Jun | Jul | Aug | Sep | Oct | Nov | Dec

Starting Balance: _____

INCOME

DATE	SOURCE	AMOUNT
	TOTAL	

This Month's Goals

- ■ _____
- ■ _____
- ■ _____
- ■ _____
- ■ _____

INCOME

DATE	DESCRIPTION	AMOUNT
	TOTAL	

BILLS & FIXED EXPENSES

DUE	DESCRIPTION	AMOUNT
	TOTAL	

DEBT

DATE	DESCRIPTION	AMOUNT
	TOTAL	

Monthly Bill Payment

OTHER BILLS & EXPENSES

PAID	BILL	DUE DATE	AMT. DUE	AMT. PAID	UNPAID BALANCE	NOTES
Total						

THIS MONTH'S FINANCIAL OVERVIEW

OPENING BALANCE	
TOTAL INCOME	
TOTAL EXPENSES	
DIFFERENCE	
TOTAL SAVINGS	
BALANCE FORWARD	

MY BIGGEST SPENDING AREA

MY SMALLEST SPENDING AREA

Month / Year: _____

| Jan | Feb | Mar | Apr | May | Jun | Jul | Aug | Sep | Oct | Nov | Dec |

Starting Balance: _____

INCOME

DATE	SOURCE	AMOUNT
	TOTAL	

This Month's Goals

- ■ _____
- ■ _____
- ■ _____
- ■ _____
- ■ _____

INCOME

DATE	DESCRIPTION	AMOUNT
	TOTAL	

BILLS & FIXED EXPENSES

DUE	DESCRIPTION	AMOUNT
	TOTAL	

DEBT

DATE	DESCRIPTION	AMOUNT
	TOTAL	

Monthly Bill Payment

PAID	BILL	DUE DATE	AMT. DUE	AMT. PAID	UNPAID BALANCE	NOTES
	Total					

THIS MONTH'S FINANCIAL OVERVIEW

OPENING BALANCE	
TOTAL INCOME	
TOTAL EXPENSES	
DIFFERENCE	
TOTAL SAVINGS	
BALANCE FORWARD	

MY BIGGEST SPENDING AREA

MY SMALLEST SPENDING AREA

Month / Year: _____ | Jan | Feb | Mar | Apr | May | Jun | Jul | Aug | Sep | Oct | Nov | Dec

Starting Balance: _____

INCOME		
DATE	SOURCE	AMOUNT
	TOTAL	

This Month's Goals

■ _____

■ _____

■ _____

■ _____

■ _____

INCOME		
DATE	DESCRIPTION	AMOUNT
	TOTAL	

BILLS & FIXED EXPENSES		
DUE	DESCRIPTION	AMOUNT
	TOTAL	

DEBT		
DATE	DESCRIPTION	AMOUNT
	TOTAL	

Monthly Bill Payment

OTHER BILLS & EXPENSES

PAID	BILL	DUE DATE	AMT. DUE	AMT. PAID	UNPAID BALANCE	NOTES
Total						

THIS MONTH'S FINANCIAL OVERVIEW

OPENING BALANCE	
TOTAL INCOME	
TOTAL EXPENSES	
DIFFERENCE	
TOTAL SAVINGS	
BALANCE FORWARD	

MY BIGGEST SPENDING AREA

MY SMALLEST SPENDING AREA

Month / Year: _____ | Jan | Feb | Mar | Apr | May | Jun | Jul | Aug | Sep | Oct | Nov | Dec

Starting Balance: _____

INCOME

DATE	SOURCE	AMOUNT
	TOTAL	

This Month's Goals

- ■ _____
- ■ _____
- ■ _____
- ■ _____
- ■ _____

INCOME

DATE	DESCRIPTION	AMOUNT
	TOTAL	

BILLS & FIXED EXPENSES

DUE	DESCRIPTION	AMOUNT
	TOTAL	

DEBT

DATE	DESCRIPTION	AMOUNT
	TOTAL	

Monthly Bill Payment

PAID	BILL	DUE DATE	AMT. DUE	AMT. PAID	UNPAID BALANCE	NOTES
	Total					

THIS MONTH'S FINANCIAL OVERVIEW

OPENING BALANCE	
TOTAL INCOME	
TOTAL EXPENSES	
DIFFERENCE	
TOTAL SAVINGS	
BALANCE FORWARD	

MY BIGGEST SPENDING AREA

MY SMALLEST SPENDING AREA

Month / Year: _____

| Jan | Feb | Mar | Apr | May | Jun | Jul | Aug | Sep | Oct | Nov | Dec |

Starting Balance: _____

INCOME

DATE	SOURCE	AMOUNT
	TOTAL	

This Month's Goals

- ■ _____
- ■ _____
- ■ _____
- ■ _____
- ■ _____

INCOME

DATE	DESCRIPTION	AMOUNT
	TOTAL	

BILLS & FIXED EXPENSES

DUE	DESCRIPTION	AMOUNT
	TOTAL	

DEBT

DATE	DESCRIPTION	AMOUNT
	TOTAL	

Monthly Bill Payment

PAID	BILL	DUE DATE	AMT. DUE	AMT. PAID	UNPAID BALANCE	NOTES
Total						

THIS MONTH'S FINANCIAL OVERVIEW

OPENING BALANCE	
TOTAL INCOME	
TOTAL EXPENSES	
DIFFERENCE	
TOTAL SAVINGS	
BALANCE FORWARD	

MY BIGGEST SPENDING AREA

MY SMALLEST SPENDING AREA

Month / Year: _____

| Jan | Feb | Mar | Apr | May | Jun | Jul | Aug | Sep | Oct | Nov | Dec |

Starting Balance: _____

INCOME

DATE	SOURCE	AMOUNT
	TOTAL	

This Month's Goals

- _____
- _____
- _____
- _____
- _____

INCOME

DATE	DESCRIPTION	AMOUNT
	TOTAL	

BILLS & FIXED EXPENSES

DUE	DESCRIPTION	AMOUNT
	TOTAL	

DEBT

DATE	DESCRIPTION	AMOUNT
	TOTAL	

Monthly Bill Payment

PAID	BILL	DUE DATE	AMT. DUE	AMT. PAID	UNPAID BALANCE	NOTES
	Total					

THIS MONTH'S FINANCIAL OVERVIEW

OPENING BALANCE	
TOTAL INCOME	
TOTAL EXPENSES	
DIFFERENCE	
TOTAL SAVINGS	
BALANCE FORWARD	

MY BIGGEST SPENDING AREA

MY SMALLEST SPENDING AREA

Month / Year: _____ | Jan | Feb | Mar | Apr | May | Jun | Jul | Aug | Sep | Oct | Nov | Dec |

Starting Balance: _____

INCOME

DATE	SOURCE	AMOUNT
	TOTAL	

This Month's Goals

- ◼ _____
- ◼ _____
- ◼ _____
- ◼ _____
- ◼ _____

INCOME

DATE	DESCRIPTION	AMOUNT
	TOTAL	

BILLS & FIXED EXPENSES

DUE	DESCRIPTION	AMOUNT
	TOTAL	

DEBT

DATE	DESCRIPTION	AMOUNT
	TOTAL	

Monthly Bill Payment

PAID	BILL	DUE DATE	AMT. DUE	AMT. PAID	UNPAID BALANCE	NOTES
	Total					

THIS MONTH'S FINANCIAL OVERVIEW

OPENING BALANCE	
TOTAL INCOME	
TOTAL EXPENSES	
DIFFERENCE	
TOTAL SAVINGS	
BALANCE FORWARD	

MY BIGGEST SPENDING AREA

MY SMALLEST SPENDING AREA

SUMMARY OF THE YEAR

MONTH	JAN	FEB	MAR	APR	APR	JUN
TOTAL INCOME						
TOTAL EXPENSES						
BALANCE						
SAVINGS						

Monthly Expenses Summary

CATEGORY	JAN	FEB	MAR	APR	APR	JUN

SUMMARY OF THE YEAR

MONTH	Jul	Aug	Sep	Oct	Nov	Dec
TOTAL INCOME						
TOTAL EXPENSES						
BALANCE						
SAVINGS						

Monthly Expenses Summary

CATEGORY	Jul	Aug	Sep	Oct	Nov	Dec

My Yearly Financial Goals

1

2

3

4

5

6

7

8

My Mind Map

Month / Year: _____

| Jan | Feb | Mar | Apr | May | Jun | Jul | Aug | Sep | Oct | Nov | Dec |

Starting Balance: _____

INCOME

DATE	SOURCE	AMOUNT
	TOTAL	

This Month's Goals

- ▪ _____
- ▪ _____
- ▪ _____
- ▪ _____
- ▪ _____

INCOME

DATE	DESCRIPTION	AMOUNT
	TOTAL	

BILLS & FIXED EXPENSES

DUE	DESCRIPTION	AMOUNT
	TOTAL	

DEBT

DATE	DESCRIPTION	AMOUNT
	TOTAL	

Monthly Bill Payment

PAID	BILL	DUE DATE	AMT. DUE	AMT. PAID	UNPAID BALANCE	NOTES
	Total					

THIS MONTH'S FINANCIAL OVERVIEW

OPENING BALANCE	
TOTAL INCOME	
TOTAL EXPENSES	
DIFFERENCE	
TOTAL SAVINGS	
BALANCE FORWARD	

MY BIGGEST SPENDING AREA

MY SMALLEST SPENDING AREA

Month / Year: _____ | Jan | Feb | Mar | Apr | May | Jun | Jul | Aug | Sep | Oct | Nov | Dec

Starting Balance: _____

INCOME

DATE	SOURCE	AMOUNT
	TOTAL	

This Month's Goals

- ■ _____
- ■ _____
- ■ _____
- ■ _____
- ■ _____

INCOME

DATE	DESCRIPTION	AMOUNT
	TOTAL	

BILLS & FIXED EXPENSES

DUE	DESCRIPTION	AMOUNT
	TOTAL	

DEBT

DATE	DESCRIPTION	AMOUNT
	TOTAL	

Monthly Bill Payment

PAID	BILL	DUE DATE	AMT. DUE	AMT. PAID	UNPAID BALANCE	NOTES
Total						

THIS MONTH'S FINANCIAL OVERVIEW

OPENING BALANCE	
TOTAL INCOME	
TOTAL EXPENSES	
DIFFERENCE	
TOTAL SAVINGS	
BALANCE FORWARD	

MY BIGGEST SPENDING AREA

MY SMALLEST SPENDING AREA

Month / Year: _____

| Jan | Feb | Mar | Apr | May | Jun | Jul | Aug | Sep | Oct | Nov | Dec |

Starting Balance: _____

INCOME

DATE	SOURCE	AMOUNT
	TOTAL	

This Month's Goals

■ _____

■ _____

■ _____

■ _____

■ _____

INCOME

DATE	DESCRIPTION	AMOUNT
	TOTAL	

BILLS & FIXED EXPENSES

DUE	DESCRIPTION	AMOUNT
	TOTAL	

DEBT

DATE	DESCRIPTION	AMOUNT
	TOTAL	

Monthly Bill Payment

OTHER BILLS & EXPENSES

PAID	BILL	DUE DATE	AMT. DUE	AMT. PAID	UNPAID BALANCE	NOTES
	Total					

THIS MONTH'S FINANCIAL OVERVIEW

OPENING BALANCE	
TOTAL INCOME	
TOTAL EXPENSES	
DIFFERENCE	
TOTAL SAVINGS	
BALANCE FORWARD	

MY BIGGEST SPENDING AREA

MY SMALLEST SPENDING AREA

Month / Year: _____

Jan Feb Mar Apr May Jun Jul Aug Sep Oct Nov Dec

Starting Balance: _____

INCOME

DATE	SOURCE	AMOUNT
	TOTAL	

This Month's Goals

- _____
- _____
- _____
- _____
- _____

INCOME

DATE	DESCRIPTION	AMOUNT
	TOTAL	

BILLS & FIXED EXPENSES

DUE	DESCRIPTION	AMOUNT
	TOTAL	

DEBT

DATE	DESCRIPTION	AMOUNT
	TOTAL	

Monthly Bill Payment

PAID	BILL	DUE DATE	AMT. DUE	AMT. PAID	UNPAID BALANCE	NOTES
	Total					

THIS MONTH'S FINANCIAL OVERVIEW

OPENING BALANCE	
TOTAL INCOME	
TOTAL EXPENSES	
DIFFERENCE	
TOTAL SAVINGS	
BALANCE FORWARD	

MY BIGGEST SPENDING AREA

MY SMALLEST SPENDING AREA

Month / Year: _____

| Jan | Feb | Mar | Apr | May | Jun | Jul | Aug | Sep | Oct | Nov | Dec |

Starting Balance: _____

INCOME

DATE	SOURCE	AMOUNT
	TOTAL	

This Month's Goals

- ■ _____
- ■ _____
- ■ _____
- ■ _____
- ■ _____

INCOME

DATE	DESCRIPTION	AMOUNT
	TOTAL	

BILLS & FIXED EXPENSES

DUE	DESCRIPTION	AMOUNT
	TOTAL	

DEBT

DATE	DESCRIPTION	AMOUNT
	TOTAL	

Monthly Bill Payment

PAID	BILL	DUE DATE	AMT. DUE	AMT. PAID	UNPAID BALANCE	NOTES
Total						

THIS MONTH'S FINANCIAL OVERVIEW

OPENING BALANCE	
TOTAL INCOME	
TOTAL EXPENSES	
DIFFERENCE	
TOTAL SAVINGS	
BALANCE FORWARD	

MY BIGGEST SPENDING AREA

MY SMALLEST SPENDING AREA

Month / Year: _____

| Jan | Feb | Mar | Apr | May | Jun | Jul | Aug | Sep | Oct | Nov | Dec |

Starting Balance: _____

INCOME

DATE	SOURCE	AMOUNT
	TOTAL	

This Month's Goals

- ■ _____
- ■ _____
- ■ _____
- ■ _____
- ■ _____

INCOME

DATE	DESCRIPTION	AMOUNT
	TOTAL	

BILLS & FIXED EXPENSES

DUE	DESCRIPTION	AMOUNT
	TOTAL	

DEBT

DATE	DESCRIPTION	AMOUNT
	TOTAL	

Monthly Bill Payment

PAID	BILL	DUE DATE	AMT. DUE	AMT. PAID	UNPAID BALANCE	NOTES
Total						

THIS MONTH'S FINANCIAL OVERVIEW

OPENING BALANCE	
TOTAL INCOME	
TOTAL EXPENSES	
DIFFERENCE	
TOTAL SAVINGS	
BALANCE FORWARD	

MY BIGGEST SPENDING AREA

MY SMALLEST SPENDING AREA

Month / Year: _____

| Jan | Feb | Mar | Apr | May | Jun | Jul | Aug | Sep | Oct | Nov | Dec |

Starting Balance: _____

INCOME

DATE	SOURCE	AMOUNT
	TOTAL	

This Month's Goals

- ■ _____
- ■ _____
- ■ _____
- ■ _____
- ■ _____

INCOME

DATE	DESCRIPTION	AMOUNT
	TOTAL	

BILLS & FIXED EXPENSES

DUE	DESCRIPTION	AMOUNT
	TOTAL	

DEBT

DATE	DESCRIPTION	AMOUNT
	TOTAL	

Monthly Bill Payment

OTHER BILLS & EXPENSES

PAID	BILL	DUE DATE	AMT. DUE	AMT. PAID	UNPAID BALANCE	NOTES
Total						

THIS MONTH'S FINANCIAL OVERVIEW

OPENING BALANCE	
TOTAL INCOME	
TOTAL EXPENSES	
DIFFERENCE	
TOTAL SAVINGS	
BALANCE FORWARD	

MY BIGGEST SPENDING AREA

MY SMALLEST SPENDING AREA

Month / Year: _____

Jan | Feb | Mar | Apr | May | Jun | Jul | Aug | Sep | Oct | Nov | Dec

Starting Balance: _____

INCOME		
DATE	SOURCE	AMOUNT
	TOTAL	

This Month's Goals
■ _____
■ _____
■ _____
■ _____
■ _____

INCOME		
DATE	DESCRIPTION	AMOUNT
	TOTAL	

BILLS & FIXED EXPENSES		
DUE	DESCRIPTION	AMOUNT
	TOTAL	

DEBT		
DATE	DESCRIPTION	AMOUNT
	TOTAL	

Monthly Bill Payment

PAID	BILL	DUE DATE	AMT. DUE	AMT. PAID	UNPAID BALANCE	NOTES
	Total					

THIS MONTH'S FINANCIAL OVERVIEW

OPENING BALANCE	
TOTAL INCOME	
TOTAL EXPENSES	
DIFFERENCE	
TOTAL SAVINGS	
BALANCE FORWARD	

MY BIGGEST SPENDING AREA

MY SMALLEST SPENDING AREA

Month / Year: _____ | Jan | Feb | Mar | Apr | May | Jun | Jul | Aug | Sep | Oct | Nov | Dec

Starting Balance: _____

INCOME

DATE	SOURCE	AMOUNT
	TOTAL	

This Month's Goals

- ■ _____
- ■ _____
- ■ _____
- ■ _____
- ■ _____

INCOME

DATE	DESCRIPTION	AMOUNT
	TOTAL	

BILLS & FIXED EXPENSES

DUE	DESCRIPTION	AMOUNT
	TOTAL	

DEBT

DATE	DESCRIPTION	AMOUNT
	TOTAL	

Monthly Bill Payment

OTHER BILLS & EXPENSES

PAID	BILL	DUE DATE	AMT. DUE	AMT. PAID	UNPAID BALANCE	NOTES
Total						

THIS MONTH'S FINANCIAL OVERVIEW

OPENING BALANCE	
TOTAL INCOME	
TOTAL EXPENSES	
DIFFERENCE	
TOTAL SAVINGS	
BALANCE FORWARD	

MY BIGGEST SPENDING AREA

MY SMALLEST SPENDING AREA

Month / Year: _____

Jan	Feb	Mar	Apr	May	Jun	Jul	Aug	Sep	Oct	Nov	Dec

Starting Balance: _____

INCOME

DATE	SOURCE	AMOUNT
	TOTAL	

This Month's Goals

- _____
- _____
- _____
- _____
- _____

INCOME

DATE	DESCRIPTION	AMOUNT
	TOTAL	

BILLS & FIXED EXPENSES

DUE	DESCRIPTION	AMOUNT
	TOTAL	

DEBT

DATE	DESCRIPTION	AMOUNT
	TOTAL	

Monthly Bill Payment

PAID	BILL	DUE DATE	AMT. DUE	AMT. PAID	UNPAID BALANCE	NOTES
Total						

THIS MONTH'S FINANCIAL OVERVIEW

OPENING BALANCE	
TOTAL INCOME	
TOTAL EXPENSES	
DIFFERENCE	
TOTAL SAVINGS	
BALANCE FORWARD	

MY BIGGEST SPENDING AREA

MY SMALLEST SPENDING AREA

Month / Year: _____ | Jan | Feb | Mar | Apr | May | Jun | Jul | Aug | Sep | Oct | Nov | Dec

Starting Balance: _____

INCOME

DATE	SOURCE	AMOUNT
	TOTAL	

This Month's Goals

- ■ _____
- ■ _____
- ■ _____
- ■ _____
- ■ _____

INCOME

DATE	DESCRIPTION	AMOUNT
	TOTAL	

BILLS & FIXED EXPENSES

DUE	DESCRIPTION	AMOUNT
	TOTAL	

DEBT

DATE	DESCRIPTION	AMOUNT
	TOTAL	

Monthly Bill Payment

PAID	BILL	DUE DATE	AMT. DUE	AMT. PAID	UNPAID BALANCE	NOTES
	Total					

THIS MONTH'S FINANCIAL OVERVIEW

OPENING BALANCE	
TOTAL INCOME	
TOTAL EXPENSES	
DIFFERENCE	
TOTAL SAVINGS	
BALANCE FORWARD	

MY BIGGEST SPENDING AREA

MY SMALLEST SPENDING AREA

Month / Year: _____

| Jan | Feb | Mar | Apr | May | Jun | Jul | Aug | Sep | Oct | Nov | Dec |

Starting Balance: _____

INCOME

DATE	SOURCE	AMOUNT
	TOTAL	

This Month's Goals

- ■ _____
- ■ _____
- ■ _____
- ■ _____
- ■ _____

INCOME

DATE	DESCRIPTION	AMOUNT
	TOTAL	

BILLS & FIXED EXPENSES

DUE	DESCRIPTION	AMOUNT
	TOTAL	

DEBT

DATE	DESCRIPTION	AMOUNT
	TOTAL	

Monthly Bill Payment

OTHER BILLS & EXPENSES

PAID	BILL	DUE DATE	AMT. DUE	AMT. PAID	UNPAID BALANCE	NOTES
Total						

THIS MONTH'S FINANCIAL OVERVIEW

OPENING BALANCE	
TOTAL INCOME	
TOTAL EXPENSES	
DIFFERENCE	
TOTAL SAVINGS	
BALANCE FORWARD	

MY BIGGEST SPENDING AREA

MY SMALLEST SPENDING AREA

Month / Year: _____

Jan | Feb | Mar | Apr | May | Jun | Jul | Aug | Sep | Oct | Nov | Dec

Starting Balance: _____

INCOME

DATE	SOURCE	AMOUNT
	TOTAL	

This Month's Goals

- ☐ _____
- ☐ _____
- ☐ _____
- ☐ _____
- ☐ _____

INCOME

DATE	DESCRIPTION	AMOUNT
	TOTAL	

BILLS & FIXED EXPENSES

DUE	DESCRIPTION	AMOUNT
	TOTAL	

DEBT

DATE	DESCRIPTION	AMOUNT
	TOTAL	

Monthly Bill Payment

OTHER BILLS & EXPENSES

PAID	BILL	DUE DATE	AMT. DUE	AMT. PAID	UNPAID BALANCE	NOTES
Total						

THIS MONTH'S FINANCIAL OVERVIEW

OPENING BALANCE	
TOTAL INCOME	
TOTAL EXPENSES	
DIFFERENCE	
TOTAL SAVINGS	
BALANCE FORWARD	

MY BIGGEST SPENDING AREA
MY SMALLEST SPENDING AREA

My Yearly Financial Goals

1

2

3

4

5

6

7

8

My Mind Map

Month / Year: _____

| Jan | Feb | Mar | Apr | May | Jun | Jul | Aug | Sep | Oct | Nov | Dec |

| Starting Balance: _____ |

INCOME

DATE	SOURCE	AMOUNT
	TOTAL	

This Month's Goals

- ■ _____
- ■ _____
- ■ _____
- ■ _____
- ■ _____

INCOME

DATE	DESCRIPTION	AMOUNT
	TOTAL	

BILLS & FIXED EXPENSES

DUE	DESCRIPTION	AMOUNT
	TOTAL	

DEBT

DATE	DESCRIPTION	AMOUNT
	TOTAL	

Monthly Bill Payment

PAID	BILL	DUE DATE	AMT. DUE	AMT. PAID	UNPAID BALANCE	NOTES
	Total					

THIS MONTH'S FINANCIAL OVERVIEW

OPENING BALANCE	
TOTAL INCOME	
TOTAL EXPENSES	
DIFFERENCE	
TOTAL SAVINGS	
BALANCE FORWARD	

MY BIGGEST SPENDING AREA

MY SMALLEST SPENDING AREA

Month / Year: _____

| Jan | Feb | Mar | Apr | May | Jun | Jul | Aug | Sep | Oct | Nov | Dec |

Starting Balance: _____

INCOME

DATE	SOURCE	AMOUNT
	TOTAL	

This Month's Goals

- ■ _____
- ■ _____
- ■ _____
- ■ _____
- ■ _____

INCOME

DATE	DESCRIPTION	AMOUNT
	TOTAL	

BILLS & FIXED EXPENSES

DUE	DESCRIPTION	AMOUNT
	TOTAL	

DEBT

DATE	DESCRIPTION	AMOUNT
	TOTAL	

Monthly Bill Payment

OTHER BILLS & EXPENSES

PAID	BILL	DUE DATE	AMT. DUE	AMT. PAID	UNPAID BALANCE	NOTES
Total						

THIS MONTH'S FINANCIAL OVERVIEW

OPENING BALANCE	
TOTAL INCOME	
TOTAL EXPENSES	
DIFFERENCE	
TOTAL SAVINGS	
BALANCE FORWARD	

MY BIGGEST SPENDING AREA

MY SMALLEST SPENDING AREA

Month / Year: ______

Jan	Feb	Mar	Apr	May	Jun	Jul	Aug	Sep	Oct	Nov	Dec

Starting Balance: ____________

INCOME

DATE	SOURCE	AMOUNT
	TOTAL	

This Month's Goals

- ____________
- ____________
- ____________
- ____________
- ____________

INCOME

DATE	DESCRIPTION	AMOUNT
	TOTAL	

BILLS & FIXED EXPENSES

DUE	DESCRIPTION	AMOUNT
	TOTAL	

DEBT

DATE	DESCRIPTION	AMOUNT
	TOTAL	

Monthly Bill Payment

OTHER BILLS & EXPENSES

PAID	BILL	DUE DATE	AMT. DUE	AMT. PAID	UNPAID BALANCE	NOTES
Total						

THIS MONTH'S FINANCIAL OVERVIEW

OPENING BALANCE	
TOTAL INCOME	
TOTAL EXPENSES	
DIFFERENCE	
TOTAL SAVINGS	
BALANCE FORWARD	

MY BIGGEST SPENDING AREA

MY SMALLEST SPENDING AREA

Month / Year: _____

| Jan | Feb | Mar | Apr | May | Jun | Jul | Aug | Sep | Oct | Nov | Dec |

Starting Balance: _____

INCOME

DATE	SOURCE	AMOUNT
	TOTAL	

This Month's Goals

- ■ _____
- ■ _____
- ■ _____
- ■ _____
- ■ _____

INCOME

DATE	DESCRIPTION	AMOUNT
	TOTAL	

BILLS & FIXED EXPENSES

DUE	DESCRIPTION	AMOUNT
	TOTAL	

DEBT

DATE	DESCRIPTION	AMOUNT
	TOTAL	

Monthly Bill Payment

OTHER BILLS & EXPENSES

PAID	BILL	DUE DATE	AMT. DUE	AMT. PAID	UNPAID BALANCE	NOTES
Total						

THIS MONTH'S FINANCIAL OVERVIEW

OPENING BALANCE	
TOTAL INCOME	
TOTAL EXPENSES	
DIFFERENCE	
TOTAL SAVINGS	
BALANCE FORWARD	

MY BIGGEST SPENDING AREA

MY SMALLEST SPENDING AREA

Month / Year: _____ | Jan | Feb | Mar | Apr | May | Jun | Jul | Aug | Sep | Oct | Nov | Dec |

Starting Balance: _____

INCOME

DATE	SOURCE	AMOUNT
	TOTAL	

This Month's Goals

- ■ _____
- ■ _____
- ■ _____
- ■ _____
- ■ _____

INCOME

DATE	DESCRIPTION	AMOUNT
	TOTAL	

BILLS & FIXED EXPENSES

DUE	DESCRIPTION	AMOUNT
	TOTAL	

DEBT

DATE	DESCRIPTION	AMOUNT
	TOTAL	

Monthly Bill Payment

OTHER BILLS & EXPENSES

PAID	BILL	DUE DATE	AMT. DUE	AMT. PAID	UNPAID BALANCE	NOTES
	Total					

THIS MONTH'S FINANCIAL OVERVIEW

OPENING BALANCE	
TOTAL INCOME	
TOTAL EXPENSES	
DIFFERENCE	
TOTAL SAVINGS	
BALANCE FORWARD	

MY BIGGEST SPENDING AREA

MY SMALLEST SPENDING AREA

Month / Year: _____

| Jan | Feb | Mar | Apr | May | Jun | Jul | Aug | Sep | Oct | Nov | Dec |

Starting Balance: _____

INCOME

DATE	SOURCE	AMOUNT
	TOTAL	

This Month's Goals

- _____
- _____
- _____
- _____
- _____

INCOME

DATE	DESCRIPTION	AMOUNT
	TOTAL	

BILLS & FIXED EXPENSES

DUE	DESCRIPTION	AMOUNT
	TOTAL	

DEBT

DATE	DESCRIPTION	AMOUNT
	TOTAL	

Monthly Bill Payment

OTHER BILLS & EXPENSES

PAID	BILL	DUE DATE	AMT. DUE	AMT. PAID	UNPAID BALANCE	NOTES
Total						

THIS MONTH'S FINANCIAL OVERVIEW

OPENING BALANCE	
TOTAL INCOME	
TOTAL EXPENSES	
DIFFERENCE	
TOTAL SAVINGS	
BALANCE FORWARD	

MY BIGGEST SPENDING AREA

MY SMALLEST SPENDING AREA

Month / Year: _____   Jan Feb Mar Apr May Jun Jul Aug Sep Oct Nov Dec

Starting Balance: _____

INCOME

DATE	SOURCE	AMOUNT
	TOTAL	

This Month's Goals

- _____
- _____
- _____
- _____
- _____

INCOME

DATE	DESCRIPTION	AMOUNT
	TOTAL	

BILLS & FIXED EXPENSES

DUE	DESCRIPTION	AMOUNT
	TOTAL	

DEBT

DATE	DESCRIPTION	AMOUNT
	TOTAL	

Monthly Bill Payment

OTHER BILLS & EXPENSES

PAID	BILL	DUE DATE	AMT. DUE	AMT. PAID	UNPAID BALANCE	NOTES
	Total					

THIS MONTH'S FINANCIAL OVERVIEW

OPENING BALANCE	
TOTAL INCOME	
TOTAL EXPENSES	
DIFFERENCE	
TOTAL SAVINGS	
BALANCE FORWARD	

MY BIGGEST SPENDING AREA

MY SMALLEST SPENDING AREA

Month / Year: _____ | Jan | Feb | Mar | Apr | May | Jun | Jul | Aug | Sep | Oct | Nov | Dec

Starting Balance: _____

INCOME

DATE	SOURCE	AMOUNT
	TOTAL	

This Month's Goals

- ▪ _____
- ▪ _____
- ▪ _____
- ▪ _____
- ▪ _____

INCOME

DATE	DESCRIPTION	AMOUNT
	TOTAL	

BILLS & FIXED EXPENSES

DUE	DESCRIPTION	AMOUNT
	TOTAL	

DEBT

DATE	DESCRIPTION	AMOUNT
	TOTAL	

Monthly Bill Payment

PAID	BILL	DUE DATE	AMT. DUE	AMT. PAID	UNPAID BALANCE	NOTES
	Total					

THIS MONTH'S FINANCIAL OVERVIEW

OPENING BALANCE	
TOTAL INCOME	
TOTAL EXPENSES	
DIFFERENCE	
TOTAL SAVINGS	
BALANCE FORWARD	

MY BIGGEST SPENDING AREA

MY SMALLEST SPENDING AREA

DEBT PAYMENT TRACKER

CREDITOR		STARTING BALANCE	
ACCOUNT #		MINIMUM PAYMENT	
INTEREST RATE		GOAL PAYOFF DATE	

DATE	AMOUNT PAID	BALANCE	NOTES

CREDITOR		STARTING BALANCE	
ACCOUNT #		MINIMUM PAYMENT	
INTEREST RATE		GOAL PAYOFF DATE	

DATE	AMOUNT PAID	BALANCE	NOTES

DEBT PAYMENT TRACKER

CREDITOR		STARTING BALANCE	
ACCOUNT #		MINIMUM PAYMENT	
INTEREST RATE		GOAL PAYOFF DATE	

DATE	AMOUNT PAID	BALANCE	NOTES

CREDITOR		STARTING BALANCE	
ACCOUNT #		MINIMUM PAYMENT	
INTEREST RATE		GOAL PAYOFF DATE	

DATE	AMOUNT PAID	BALANCE	NOTES

Notes

Made in United States
Troutdale, OR
09/26/2024

23170304R00064